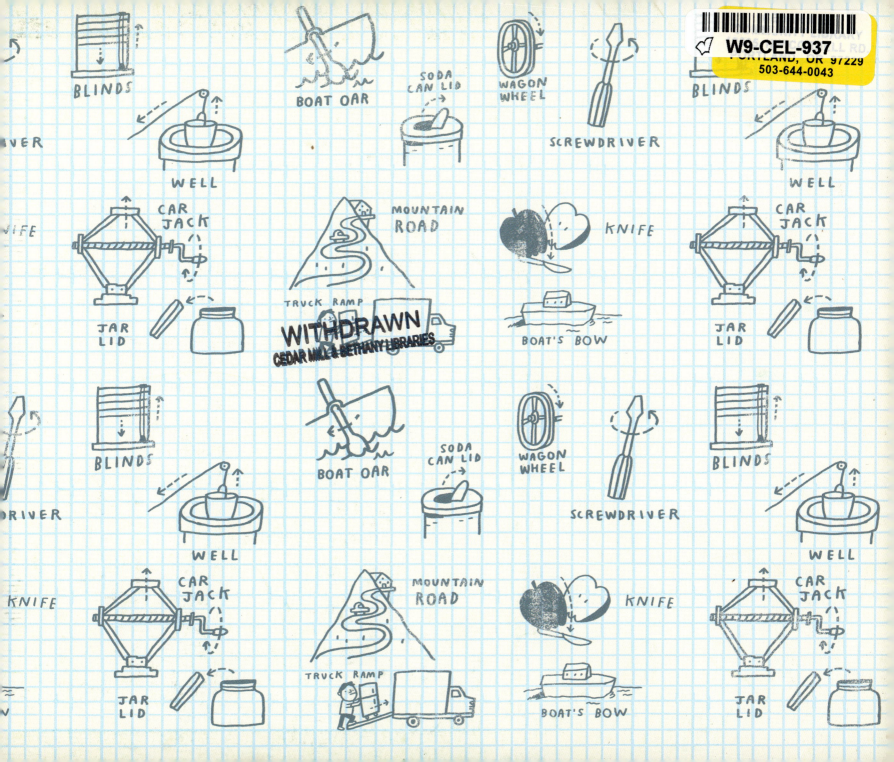

SIMPLE MACHINES

BY D. J. WARD · ILLUSTRATED BY MIKE LOWERY

HARPER

An Imprint of HarperCollinsPublishers

Special thanks to Dr. Babatunde A. Ogunnaike, William L. Friend Chaired Professor of Chemical Engineering and Dean, College of Engineering, at the University of Delaware, for his valuable assistance.

The Let's-Read-and-Find-Out Science book series was originated by Dr. Franklyn M. Branley, Astronomer Emeritus and former Chairman of the American Museum of Natural History–Hayden Planetarium, and was formerly co-edited by him and Dr. Roma Gans, Professor Emeritus of Childhood Education, Teachers College, Columbia University. Text and illustrations for each of the books in the series are checked for accuracy by an expert in the relevant field. For more information about Let's-Read-and-Find-Out Science books, write to HarperCollins Children's Books, 195 Broadway, New York, NY 10007, or visit our website at www.letsreadandfindout.com.

Let's Read-and-Find-Out Science® is a trademark of HarperCollins Publishers.

Library of Congress Cataloging-in-Publication Data
Ward, D. J. (David John), date.
 Simple machines / by D. J. Ward ; illustrated by Mike Lowery. — First edition.
  pages cm — (Let's-read-and-find-out science. Level 2)
 Audience: 4–8.
 Audience: K to 3.
 ISBN 978-0-06-232148-0 (hardcover) — ISBN 978-0-06-232147-3 (pbk.)
 1. Simple machines—Juvenile literature. I. Lowery, Mike, date– illustrator. II. Title.
 TJ147.W38 2015   2014041197
 621.8—dc23   CIP
                                                                                                          AC

The artist used pen and ink and digital media to create the digital illustrations for this book.
Typography by Erica De Chavez
15 16 17 18 19 SCP 10 9 8 7 6 5 4 3 2 1
❖
First Edition

Have you ever had to move something really heavy? How did you do it?

9

Or did you use a machine? With a machine, you don't have to lift or push or pull so hard. Machines make work easier.

That's why machines are everywhere! Look around your neighborhood. We use machines to help us get around. Machines help us dig and build and knock things down. They help us reach way up high.

Cars, bulldozers, and lawn mowers are machines with lots of moving parts. But not all machines are so complicated. Some are so simple that you might not even think of them as machines.

BEEP BEEP

They are called **simple machines**.

Six Simple Machines

1. Lever

2. Wheel and Axle

3. Pulley

4. Ramp

5. Wedge

6. Screw

Think about a seesaw. You sit on one end of a long board. Your friend sits on the other side.

UP I GO!

The board rests on something in the middle that lets each end tip up and down. By pushing down on your end of the board, you can make your friend go up.

Have you ever tried to lift your friend without using a seesaw? It's hard, isn't it? The seesaw makes lifting your friend easier. It's a simple machine!

Lever

The seesaw is a simple machine called a **lever**. All levers have two parts.

1 The first part is a board or a rod that won't bend or break easily.

2 The other part is something that will let the lever turn or tip. This is called the **fulcrum**.

When you push down on one end of a seesaw, the other end goes up. When your end lifts up, the other side goes down.

But imagine instead if
your mom or dad were on
the other side. They weigh
much more than you do. It
would be very hard to make
them go up. You might get
stuck high off the ground!

But if we change the
seesaw, you can lift them!

BOARD

Move the fulcrum closer to your mom or dad so there is more of the board on your side. Push down on the long side. The closer the fulcrum is to your mom or dad, the easier they will be to lift.

If you have a long enough lever, you could even lift an elephant!

FULCRUM

HOME RUN!

Levers are not only good for making us stronger. They can also help us make things go faster. Pick up a stick and wave it back and forth in the air. Can you see that the end of the stick moves very fast? You are using the stick as a lever and your wrist as the fulcrum. You move your wrist a little and the end of the stick moves a lot.

Baseball bats work this way. With a twist of your wrist, you make the end of the bat move really fast. Hit the ball with a fast-moving bat and the ball goes fast too.

A lever is one kind of simple machine, but there are more.

Wheel & Axle

For instance, a doorknob is a simple machine called a **wheel and axle**. A wheel and axle is a wheel with a rod sticking out of the middle.

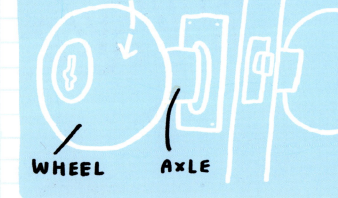

WHEEL   AXLE

When you turn the wheel, the rod turns too. The wheel is there to make the rod easier to turn.

A steering wheel is another wheel and axle. The steering wheel is connected to a rod. When you turn the steering wheel, it turns the rod. The rod steers your front wheels where you want them to go.

But what if your car didn't have a steering wheel? What if you had to steer by grabbing the rod and trying to twist it? It wouldn't be easy, that's for sure.

WHEEL

AXLE

Pulley

What would you do if you had to lift something way up high—even higher than you could reach? You might use a simple machine called a **pulley**. A pulley is a wheel with a groove in it.

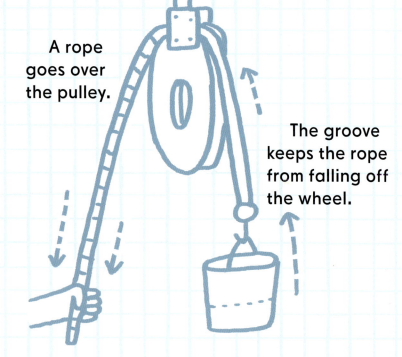

A rope goes over the pulley.

The groove keeps the rope from falling off the wheel.

As you pull the rope down on one side of the pulley, the rope goes up on the other side.

Have you ever seen someone raise a flag up a flagpole?

PULLEY →

← PULLEY

PULLEY

There is a pulley at the top of the pole. The flag is attached to a rope that hangs over the pulley. When the person pulls down on one side of the rope, the flag is pulled up the other side. That is easier than climbing up the pole!

23

Used in groups, pulleys can help you lift things much heavier than flags. The more pulleys you use, the easier it is to lift something. With enough pulleys, you could lift a rhinoceros!

Groups of pulleys lift you
when you ride in an elevator.

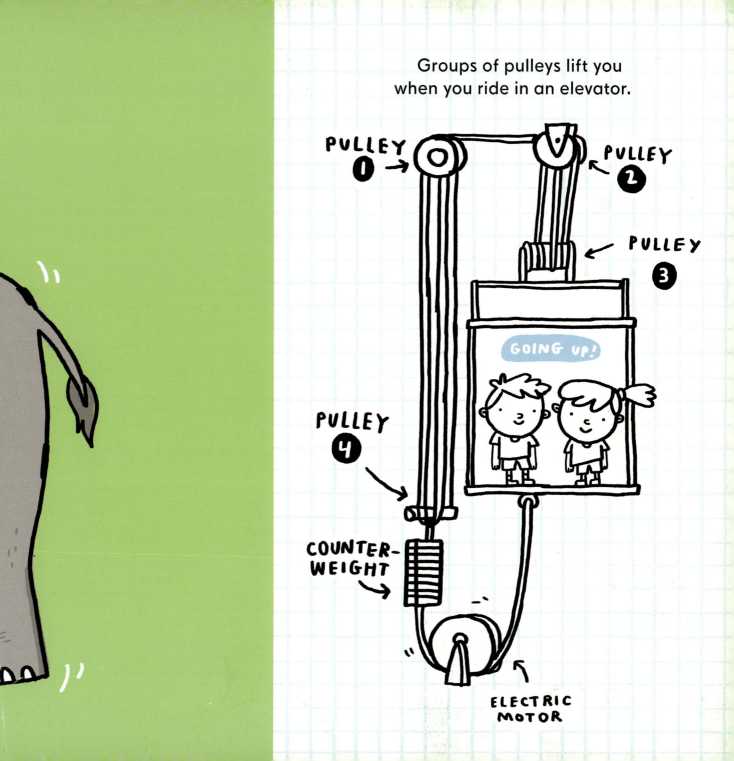

PULLEY 1 →

PULLEY 2 ←

PULLEY 3 ←

GOING UP!

PULLEY 4 →

COUNTER-
WEIGHT →

ELECTRIC
MOTOR

Ladders can be fun to climb. But what if you had to use one anytime you wanted to go up or down? You would get tired from climbing ladders all day. Instead, we use stairs, which make going up or down easier! Stairs are a kind of simple machine called a **ramp**, or an **inclined plane**.

As you go up a ramp, you are not just going up; you are also going forward at the same time. That takes much less energy than going straight up. The lower the **angle** of the ramp, the easier it is to climb.

The pyramids in Egypt were built thousands of years ago. They were made by stacking many large blocks of stone one upon another. Back then, there were no cranes for lifting such heavy things.

Guess how Egyptians got heavy stone blocks up so high? They used ramps!

27

Imagine a tall, round birthday cake. Then imagine you get a big slice of the cake! Yum! Lying on your plate, it looks like a ramp, doesn't it? Now imagine you flip the piece of cake over. It still looks like a ramp. That's because it has a ramp on both sides.

Wedge

An object with a ramp on both sides is another kind of simple machine called a **wedge**. Simple-machine wedges are made of hard materials, though, not cake!

WEDGE

An axhead is a wedge. Have you ever seen anyone chop a log with an ax? When the person swings the axhead down onto the log, the metal wedge pushes apart the wood. It splits the log. Wedges help us split things or push things apart.

Screw

Did you ever look closely at a **screw**? Through a magnifying glass, a screw looks like a tiny ramp, except the ramp twists around as it goes up.

Believe it or not, a screw is a simple machine! It's a ramp with a twist.

Not all screws are so tiny. As you walk up a spiral staircase, you walk up and go around at the same time. Some parking garages have driveways that spiral up to higher levels. These are big examples of screws.

Sometimes, to get a job done, it's best to work as a team. When a team of simple machines work together, they become a **compound machine**. Compound machines can do a job even more easily than one simple machine can.

THE MOVING DUDES

In fact, most machines you see each day are compound machines. They can be as simple as a pair of scissors or as complex as a car!

You might not be building a pyramid. You might not want to lift an elephant. Even so, simple machines are good to have around.

You might want to open your door. Turn the wheel and axle! You might ride your bike down the street. Just pedal those levers! Or you might want to help your family do some work around the house. That's great! You could use a simple machine for that. Simple machines make work easier, after all.

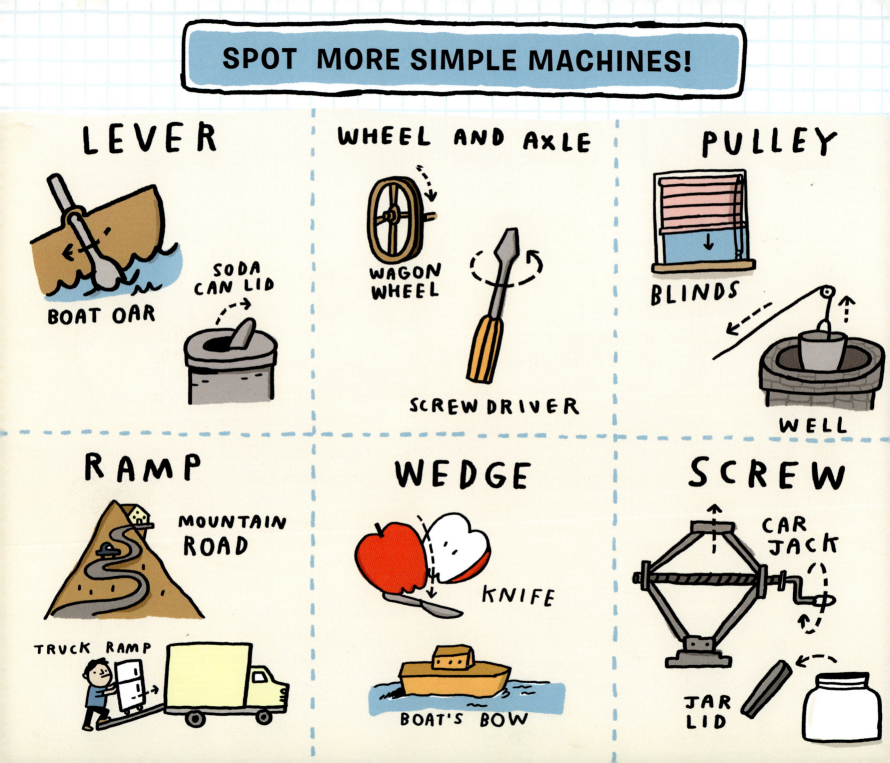

SPOT MORE SIMPLE MACHINES!

LEVER
BOAT OAR

SODA CAN LID

WHEEL AND AXLE
WAGON WHEEL

SCREWDRIVER

PULLEY
BLINDS

WELL

RAMP
MOUNTAIN ROAD

TRUCK RAMP

WEDGE
KNIFE

BOAT'S BOW

SCREW
CAR JACK

JAR LID

Glossary

Angle: The amount of steepness of a line or ramp.

Compound machine: Two or more simple machines working together.

Fulcrum: The point or object that a lever tips on or turns around.

Inclined plane: A flat surface that is tipped up at an angle; also known as a ramp.

Lever: A rod or board that can pivot back and forth or up and down.

Pulley: A grooved wheel that can spin freely on its axle; a rope or cable goes in the groove.

Ramp: A flat surface that is tipped up at an angle; also known as an inclined plane.

Screw: A spiral-shaped ramp.

Simple machine: A basic device that allows you to do work more easily than you could without the device.

Wedge: Two ramps connected to make a V shape.

Wheel and axle: A wheel attached to a rod (an axle) so that these two parts turn together.

Seesaw Cents

Materials:

- Rectangular pencil eraser (such as a "pinky" eraser)
- 12-inch wooden or hard plastic ruler
- 20 pennies

1. Set the eraser on its long, narrow edge on a level table or desk.
2. Place the ruler across the eraser so it looks like a seesaw and can rock back and forth. The ruler now is a lever, and the eraser is its fulcrum. The 6-inch mark of the ruler should be right above the eraser. This means that half the ruler is on each side of the eraser. The ruler should be able to balance this way, but if it can't, you can move it a little to the left or right until it balances.
3. Place two pennies on one end of the ruler. When you put them on, the ruler will tip toward that side. Now put two pennies on the other side. When you do this, the ruler should tip back and balance again. The pennies are pushing down the same amount on both sides of the ruler. Since the ruler is the same length on each side, having the same amount of push on each side will make it balance. This is like when you and your friend are on a seesaw.
4. Carefully lift the ruler and move it so the 5-inch mark is now on top of the eraser. Will it balance with two pennies on each side anymore? Probably not. The longer side will go down. Where will you have to add pennies to make it balance? Add pennies—one at a time—to the shorter side of the ruler until it balances again. How many does it take? Two pennies on the longer side can balance four, five, or even six pennies on the short side.
5. Now carefully move the ruler so the 4-inch mark is over the eraser. Keep two pennies on the long side. Add pennies to the short side until it balances again. How many pennies did it take this time? Two pennies can balance a whole stack of pennies on the other side if the fulcrum is close to the stack.

This experiment shows how you can lift heavy things using a lever. If the fulcrum is much closer to the heavy thing than it is to you, it won't take a big push on your side to lift up the other side. Now you just need to find that elephant to lift!

Center of Science and Industry (Columbus, OH):
www.cosi.org/downloads/activities/simplemachines/sm1.html

Museum of Science and Industry (Chicago, IL):
www.msichicago.org/online-science/simple-machines/
activities/simple-machines-1

Be sure to look for all of these books in the LET'S-READ-AND-FIND-OUT SCIENCE series: